Words of the Awakened Mind

Zensho W. Kopp

Words of the Awakened Mind

Aphorisms of a
Western Zen Master

The Author

Zensho W. Kopp is one of the most important spiritual masters of the present. His holistic perspective of East-West mysticism opens up a contemporary path to spiritual realisation for the spiritual seeker.
He is the direct Dharma successor to Zen Master Soji Enku (1908-1977) and the author of various Zen books. Zensho leads the Tao Chan Zen Center in Wiesbaden, Germany and instructs a large group of students.

Translation © 2012 by John Kitching
Original title "Worte eines Erwachten"
Published by Schirner Verlag, Darmstadt 2008

Producer and publisher: Books on Demand GmbH, Norderstedt
Cover motive: painting by Zensho W. Kopp
Cover design: Michel Schmidt
Typesetting: Torsten Zander

Visit our website at
www.tao-chan.org

ISBN: 978-3-8482-4134-7

Preface

This little book is meant as a constant everyday companion, to help us live in the present moment of Now and to find our way back to our original true being.

The book has no beginning, no middle and no end and therefore, it is unimportant where we start to read. Wherever we open it we encounter sayings of enlightened clarity and timeless wisdom, which touch us at our most deepest. Zensho's words are simple, and at the same time profound. They come directly from the heart, from the rich treasure of his own experience.

We recommend the reader to immerse himself completely in the aphorisms of this enlightened master. And when he reads this book again and again, his understanding of it will reach new, higher levels. Between the lines, he will read that which is beyond all words, for he will be coming ever closer to the reality of his true being.

Wiesbaden, January 2008
Tao Chan Zen Center   The editors

Inner Certitude

Everything that has a beginning is subject to the laws of impermanence simply because it has a beginning.

Thus, human life too undergoes the process of birth, aging, sickness, pain and death. It is subject to the continual process of change: coming into being and passing away, coming into being and passing away.

And so we start to ask ourselves: Is that really all there is? Surely somewhere there must be something lasting? And just this alone; our desire for stability, bliss, and security is a constant indication of the presence of a higher reality.

It is this inner certainty, this inner knowledge imparted to us of our immortal divine nature.

Longing

The greater our awareness of the impermanence of all being, the more this brings forth in us the desire for liberation. This desire can then become so intensive that it no longer leaves room for any other desire.

In Indian tradition we hear of the student who, having just had his head plunged into the Ganges by his master is then asked what he was thinking of under water and was barely able to reply with the words, "air, air".

Thereupon the master said, "As long as your longing for God is not as great as your longing for air was just now under water, you will never experience God."

Complete Surrender

Spiritual desire is a calling of the Eternal; a longing from within the depths of the heart. It is a calling of the soul for the Divine, with the willingness to surrender oneself.

Complete surrender means nothing other than devoting everything to the Divine, to lay forth everything one is and has and to insist on nothing, whether it be fond ideas, wishes and habits, or anything else besides.

To surrender to the divine means to renounce one's own self-made, ego-controlled limitations, and to permit the all-powerful essence of the One Mind to take possession of us.

The greater the intensity of the longing, the greater the surrender. Yet without this longing, we will never be capable of that all-consuming love which reaches its zenith in an absolute surrender to the Divine.

Grasping for Happiness

Most of a person's life is plagued by a specific or undefined desire for this or that, all for the sake of grasping a short moment of fleeting happiness. People have the tendency of confusing happiness with pleasure, without realising that pleasure is just an illusion, a shadow of happiness.

Most people spend their whole lives in this delusion, constantly on the lookout for new pleasures. Yet everything is fleeting and cannot bring us lasting, true happiness.

Consequently, true happiness can only be found in the Everlasting; only in that which is independent of space and time.

Tantric Transformation

Transformation in the sense of Tantra means consciously and heedfully entering into what you are doing at the present moment so that you become completely one with it.

The Tantric way of transformation, the way of transforming energy is thus about using your sexual energy and learning how to turn it into spiritual energy.

Your attention should be undivided during sexual union. Forget yourselves, totally immerse yourselves in the sensual experience, for at this moment nothing else is important, whatever it may be.

Be entirely present and forget that a world exists beyond the two of you. Surrender yourselves completely and dissolve into each other.

Tantric Love

The experience of bliss in the average sexual union is, if present at all, disappointingly brief and often limited to a short moment of orgasm.

In the Tantric love act, however, this experience can be extended over a longer period of time. What previously was no more than a brief, fleeting moment of pleasurable feeling now becomes a profound inner experience of great intensity and deep peace.

And thus it activates a great amount of spiritual energy so that the love act lifts you up to an entirely new, higher plane of mystical consciousness.

Here, it is essential that you truly, completely immerse yourselves in the present moment if the sexual union is to raise you above mere bodily pleasures. Then for you both, the love act will become a mutual crossing over into a wonderful, higher dimension.

The Dynamic Nature of the Mind

The omnipresence of the One Mind pervades the entire universe.

All change and transformation is the continuous self-evolvement and self-transformation of this Universal Mind; it is the process of becoming aware of the inexpressible divine original root. Thus, the entire endless multiplicity of the external world of phenomena is the manifestation of this one all-encompassing Mind and the universe is its revelation.

Everything is in unceasing motion, which ultimately takes place only in the mind.

Our True Being

In the darkness of the heart, at our innermost, there shines a brilliant light that, like an eternal flame, lights up the whole universe.

This, our true being, is the underlying reality at the base of all our experiences. It neither comes nor goes, it is omnipresent, silent and pure, and beyond space and time. As the pure original source of all being it is unborn and indestructible.

The Awakened One

He who has awakened to the true nature of the Mind is beyond life and death, and as such, the question of "to be or not to be" has lost its meaning for him. There is no more reason for him to cling to life. Since he has recognised the wonderful unity of life and death he is beyond all duality and individual limitations.

He abides in the great affirmation and fullness of life for, having died into the mystical death, he has experienced his rebirth as awakened being from the dream of birth and death.

His liberation from the shadowy darkness of Maya has transformed his state of obscuration of the mind into the enlightened state of the boundless transcendent Mind.

Prayer of Silence

That which exists concealed at our innermost depths lies in silence and tranquillity, and in this peace of the depths of divine origin there flows the eternal, inexhaustible original source of all existence. Many words confuse the mind, yet where words are silent, the Eternal begins.

This silence in the face of the Eternal is a mystical prayer of stillness in which, at our innermost selves, in the "inner chamber of the heart" we listen closely to Him who speaks to us in concealment.

Perceiving the Eternal

To perceive the eternal Origin of Being as our inner-most true self we must firstly bring everything to an absolute silence and let go of everything that is not God.

This means no less than turning away from all external things and turning inwards to our hidden original being.

It is a turning from the external, the realm of opposites, to the internal, the all-embracing wholeness of divine being. It is a hearkening to the inexhaustible divine depths. It is the perception of the Eternal in ourselves.

Restless Thinking

The relentless tide of thoughts belongs to human nature. One thought follows the next and they move within their self-made limitations.

As a result of this restless thinking, brought about by waves and impressions on the surface of the consciousness, it is no longer possible to perceive in ourselves the omnipresent truth beyond space and time.

Our discriminating conceptual thinking must be silent if we wish to hear the divine word that speaks itself at the base of our heart.

Brain Research

Most people are of the opinion that the mind is nothing more than the result of brain activity within the bony shell of their skull.

Many brain researchers are entirely convinced that our brain produces the mind by means of complex neurological processes. As such, these materialistic-thinking rationalists view the mind as being merely the result of biochemical processes in the brain cells.

However, in truth, it is quite the opposite. The brain is nothing more than a material compaction of spiritual energy, and therefore the mind is not the result but the "cause" of all being and thus of brain activity too.

Leap into the Great Void

It is never a question of suppressing thought but much rather of surpassing thought.

For only he who, in his spiritual wrestling, has reached the boundaries of thought, is able to risk the leap into the great void.

It is the leap into the immeasurable ultimate ground of divine being.

When we rid ourselves of all conceptual thought in this way, our true self in all its glory reveals itself and we have returned to the source of all being.

Religious Symbols

Clinging to external forms and pious exercises is one of the greatest dangers on the spiritual path. These are bonds which tie us to signs and symbols which are actually meant to be no more than guideposts to point us the way inwards. Each religious symbol thus points beyond itself to what lies beyond all that can be named and portrayed.

Consequently, to go beyond religious symbols and signs does not mean to reject them but rather to aim to reach that which they point to. And just as they can be an aid to us they can also lead us to our doom. This happens when we do not move on from the signs and symbols and mistakenly believe them to be that which lies beyond all that which is nameable and conceivable.

Pallbearer

An austere person who skulks through life with a face like a pallbearer can never become enlightened. Cramped austerity is a completely erroneous attitude to life.

A humourless, austere attitude of mind is always the result of conditioned, ego-enslaved problem-thinking.

Whoever goes around frightened and tense as the victim of excessive worrying need not be surprised when their negative attitude is reflected by their surroundings and perceived by others as rejection.

It is this frightened state of mind which constructs all sorts of barriers and inhibitions between people, such that they cannot recognise their original con-substantiality.

It is fear that prevents a person from encountering another, filled with love and compassion, since the small, limited "I" dreads opening itself to the boundless expanse of the One Mind. This fear is the cause of mistrust, envy and jealousy; it turns the "I" into a fortress in the face of everything that surrounds it.

Excessive Worrying

Excessive worrying is a malady of the conditioned, worldly-bound person, who, by lacking in trust in God, attempts to shape his own destiny.

Filled with fear, he looks into the future, and melancholic or with a sense of guilt, he looks into the past. This disquiets the human heart and disperses spiritual awareness so that a person loses his ability to perceive the constant presence of the Divine Being.

Separated from the divine truth, his existence is thus no more than a lamentable shadow of what his life could be and should be. Since he no longer hears the harmonic tones of life he is only able to perceive disharmony in the world.

Consubstantiality

The prerequisite for an inner readiness to open our hearts to all beings is selfless concern and sympathetic love for all living beings which is consummated on the spiritual path.

However, this can only take place by overcoming our own conditionings to the point where we transcend the world of opposites and experience consubstantiality with all beings. Only in this way do we find true peace in ourselves and thus place love, tolerance and peace in the world.

Now

When I speak of Now there is the danger that you will turn this Now into an empty concept and say, "I must first achieve this Now". In this way, you have shifted Now into the future and have missed its absolute presentness.

You can only experience Now when you make it clear to yourself and clearly recognise: Now is already here! Never say that you must first achieve Now because Now is always here. Now is always here but "you" are not here. Now is always present, only you are not present.

Spiritual Aids

All religions and all philosophies tell you that you must do this and that: practise asceticism, study philosophical texts and commentaries, perform meditation for hours on end, and much more besides.

Many spiritual seekers use these and other methods in their efforts to achieve realisation. And most of them are so in love with one of these spiritual aids that it becomes a means unto itself, and finally a great obstacle on the path to liberation. Zen has nothing to do with all these artificial methods. With utmost emphasis it always points solely to the original state of your being – directly and immediately.

Dog Bones

Just as a dog loves to chew on its bone, your intellect loves to sink its teeth into problems. You are convinced of being the master of your intellect, but this is a terrible misconception.

It is not you who uses the intellect, but rather the intellect that uses you.

Brain Acrobat

All of the wise sayings that you have had in your head your whole life will be of no use to you whatsoever when you are lying on your deathbed. The more you pile up philosophical knowledge and cling to it, the further you distance yourself from the truth of Zen.

In the end, you are no more than a farcical brain acrobat with an immense collection of intellectual rubbish, devoid of all practical value.

Passing Clouds

Your thoughts and notions which pass across the Self-Mind have no reality, no stability; they simply pass by. They are like passing clouds which can do no other than to dissipate at some point in time.

Just as the evening clouds pass across the moon, so do the clouds of your discriminating thought pass by across the Self-Mind. And thus it can happen when you look up into the cloudy sky in the evening and do not see the moon you say: "there is no moon there today".

Yet the moon is always there, only you are not there, that is the whole problem.

Seeing Through Projections

You yourself project this entire theatre-world, this entire dream world, just as you perceive it. This is also true for all you experience in bardo, the intermediate state between death and rebirth, as described in the Tibetan Book of the Dead. All of it is just self-caused projections of the samsaric consciousness.

Yet the moment you perceive that all phenomena are your own projections you will experience your ascent above the dark haze of phenomena into the clear light of reality.

Then you will realise that your own mind and the boundless expanse of the One Mind are a single being, beside which nothing else exists.

Entanglement

When you interpret things in your own way with your intellect, you distance yourself more and more from the truth of Zen. Zen can never be made the object of logical deliberations and explanations. Instead, to really understand its truth, it must be lived within us at our innermost.

Whoever does not grasp this, and believes that he can comprehend the profound truth of Zen with his intellect, will only end up blocking his path to liberation.

You are just searching in circles. You search and analyse, prodding here and there in the hope of finding something after all. You believe that somewhere out there, there is indeed a great philosophical realisation which comes from outwards and makes the matter clear.

Yet the result is that you become increasingly caught up in the entanglement of your discriminating, conceptual thinking.

Who Am I

The sole cause of your whole problem is that you have forgotten who you are. Indeed, if you had not forgotten, you would not have come here.

You come here and ask me "Who am I?" How peculiar indeed. The wave asks the ocean: "Who am I?" And the ocean answers: "You are me!" All of you are the ocean. You yourselves are the reality you seek.

Thought, with its conceptual fixation causes discrimination, and consequently, the illusion of multiplicity appears. But where there is multiplicity, at the same time there is also separateness. You experience yourselves as separated from the whole and thus all discrimination and the myriad problems arise.

Wrong Meditation

If you cling to pleasant beatific feelings, at some point the moment will inevitably come when the pleasant feeling changes and turns in the other direction. It becomes the opposite of what it was, and then you are in a negative frame of mind.

This quietistic meditation form of beatific feelings is like a drug. It can become an addiction. Yet each time when the pleasant feelings change and turn around you begin to suffer. You experience a little joy, but then you fall into the opposite state. In so doing you are more and more a prisoner of your self-created world of opposites.

If you cling to this false form of meditation, you will never be able to accomplish your original true being and achieve liberation.

Thunder of Silence

As long as you seek the truth using your intellect you can never go beyond it. To go beyond it you must free yourself from the intellect, together with its entire collection of intellectual rubbish.

That is why there is only one sole way for you to experience the truth and that is: Free yourself of everything, whatever it may be, and the boundless expanse of the One Mind reveals itself to you as the "Thunderclap in a clear blue sky"!

It is the thunder of silence, which shakes the whole universe. The veil of maya, which was blocking your view of perceiving your original true self for countless incarnations, tears right through from top to bottom and reveals the Holy of Holies which was concealed behind it.

Naming Aids

Each conceptual designation is just a naming aid which remains caught in the discrimination of conceptual thought.

When I say, "This is a staff," and ask, "Where is top and bottom?," the problem already lies in the term "staff". But top and bottom need not bother us at all. We should not allow ourselves to be vexed by top and bottom.

Even when I just say, "This is a staff," it is already wrong. Indeed, I could also say it is a cow. Why should it not be a cow? Why should it not be an old broom or a wonderfully fragrant bouquet of flowers?

True Words

"True words are not pleasant and pleasant words are not true," says the ancient Taoist Master Lao-tse.

The deeper a master's statement is and the more it directly hits the heart of the matter, the less these are uplifting words in terms of common understanding, for they always tear the fundament of your ego-armour from beneath your feet. Whatever gives you apparent security in this space-time dimension of samsara madness all dissolves away.

Accepting Death

An understanding of the unavoidable transience of all being is the fundamental prerequisite to gaining a higher spiritual perception.

Whoever suppresses the truth of the fact that he must die remains caught in his ignorance, such that he falls prey to the surface-pull of this world.

Whoever lives as though there were no death, for him, the profound secret of his true being remains concealed. Whoever seeks the Outlasting only in the dimensions of space and time, and misunderstands death as just a mere contradiction to his life in space and time, will find no access to the true life, which lies hidden behind the truth of death.

Only he who does not bury his head in the sand but instead welcomes death can feel the great life which death points to.

Death

There is no death in the sense in which people believe it to be. Death is just a transition, just a change of scene. It is not the case that you die, and the world, together with everything that you love remains behind and you dissolve into nothing – in fact it is just the opposite.

The world dies, together with all that is familiar to you. The entire world, everything you like or dislike and everything you can perceive all dissolve away.

And now comes the crux of the matter: you yourself, in your immortal true being, remain. That is the decisive point. Everything falls away, and you remain.

Lip Service

True religious life is no spurious lip-service, as practised by some religious institutions whereby you simply avow your faith and forthwith receive your share in redemption.

It would be no different from you now saying, "Oh, I'm so hungry, my stomach is rumbling." And I say, "There's plenty of sausage and cheese in the refrigerator and there's also fresh bread. Do you believe that?" And you say, "Yes." Then I say: "Good, then you are redeemed from your hunger." It would amount to exactly the same thing.

It is just the same in superficial, dogmatic forms of religion since they revolve solely around an external belief or lip-service. You believe in the dogma and now you are saved. Great!

Cave of the Heart

Only when you have completely rid yourself of all external and internal compulsions, that is, of all patterns of conduct and thought models, will the unspeakable secret of God's birth at the base of the soul reveal itself.

This ground of the soul, as the Christian mystics call it, is man's innermost self. It is the centre of our being and the origin of all life.

It is the "cave of divine darkness", the krypta of the heart, in which the light of our true being lights up the entire universe like the sun and reveals itself to us when we behold the hidden depths.

This temple of the Holy Spirit is the "Guha Hridaya"; the cave of the heart of the Upanishads, which, as man's innermost sanctum, contains the unborn divine light.

World-Dream

Everything that causes you problems in everyday life has nothing whatsoever to do with a negative external world; with the imperfection of the world.

Stop seeking in external events for the cause of your suffering! In truth, the cause of your suffering lies within you.

You yourself are the cause of everything that happens to you and everything you encounter. It is your own projections and nothing more. And here, there is no difference, absolutely no difference at all between your daily experiences of a three-dimensional world and the world you experience at night when you sleep.

Everything you experience in this world-dream: this whole backdrop, the landscape, the creatures, all the problems, joy and suffering, coming and going, birth and death – everything, whatever it may be, you project it all yourself.

Suffering

Suffering does not come from outside – it always comes from inside, for the impermanence of all your pleasant experiences in the world can never cause suffering in you if you do not cling to them.

When you wish to hold on to something you find pleasant, and it takes leave of you, then suffering always results.

Yet the thing itself does not cause you any suffering. Solely the attachment to impermanent things causes suffering. For attachment is solidification, hardening, and hardening is always rigidification, non-movement. It is contrary to the flow of Tao.

Digressing

Just imagine: you are feeling great, you are contented with yourself and the world, and are lacking not the least thing. Suddenly, for no reason, a memory surfaces from which you now are not able to free yourself. Thought associations arise that lead to a series of emotional impulses, and before you know it, you are depressed, melancholic, or full of aggression. You are in your self-created hell.

Yet externally, nothing has changed at all; it all takes place solely within you. You yourself project the world you experience.

Futile Effort

You cannot achieve your true being, the unborn One Mind, since there is nothing to achieve.

It is just like the man who stands at the gates of paradise and tries to enter. At first he knocks tentatively, then a little harder but the gates do not open. Then he pounds with his fist, but nothing happens.

Despairingly, he kicks the gates, then, with a run up, he runs against them, all without success.

He continues his attempts throughout the night until at last, he collapses to the ground, realising that all his attempts were in vain. Yet lo and behold, the gates open, but in the opposite direction – namely towards him.

That is it! All your seeking and all your efforts to reach the unreachable do nothing other than to push shut the gates to liberation.

Limited Perspectives

Everyone has their very special perspective, their very particular understanding of the spiritual texts they study, of what they read or hear. Yet these are always just very limited perspectives.

All theories and conclusions constructed by the intellect are always limited and wrong. They are tied to discriminating, conceptual thought and thus to its narrow limits.

The intellect cannot be free from preconceived ideas since it itself is made up solely of preconceived ideas. Using conceptual logic to understand the truth is nothing more than ignorance in the eyes of Zen.

Relying on one's discriminating, conceptual thinking means preventing the inner light from unfolding.

The Cheerfulness of the Mind

When the weather is cheerful and fine, no dark clouds hang in the sky. Cheerful means light and clear. Light and clear is the original state of the mind. That is our true being, beyond the clouds of discriminating thought.

The tranquil cheerfulness of the mind, as our true original state, is constantly present.

It is solely a question of immersing ourselves in the tranquil cheerfulness of the mind by simply letting it happen. Then true life reveals itself to us. Then and only then does life become true life.

Life is Now

True life only reveals itself when we live it, and we only live it when we truly immerse ourselves in it. Life is only possible in Here and Now, for it takes place in the present moment.

If we wish to have a contented, happy life, then there is no other way than to live each moment of everyday life in deep awareness. For the meaning of all life is that you truly live. Living life means: Life is not yesterday, life is not tomorrow, life is "now"!

Complete Freedom

The true man of Zen goes into town, among the people and lives the truth of Zen in the midst of everyday life in the world.

Free and independent, he comes and goes just as he pleases. And why is this so? It is so because he is not a slave of conditionings and patterns of behaviour. Thus he need not withdraw himself from the world. Quite the contrary: he moves in the midst of the world of phenomena in complete freedom. Like the wind in the trees and the moon in the water he is constantly in clear accordance with everything. His mind is completely free from coming and going, without limits, and clings to nothing.

Baptism by Fire of the Mind

The Enlightenment experience is the great turning point in a person's life, which touches his whole personality.

He experiences a spiritual revolution, a tremendous "baptism by fire of the mind", which completely transforms his whole life. Through this rebirth he reaches a new and entirely different state of being which changes his whole perspective and his attitude to life.

Yet this experience does not only influence his mental attitude to things, rather it transforms his whole consciousness into a profound and all-encompassing understanding of life.

He who by virtue of Enlightenment has awakened to his true, divine self fulfils through this experience the true purpose of his human existence.

Worthless Toilet Paper

All Buddhist teachings, as expounded in the sutras and shastras, are in the eyes of the old Zen masters nothing more than worthless toilet paper, there to wipe up the refuse of the intellect.

Zen has nothing to do with the quibblings of philosophical deliberations and logical conclusions.

For this reason, Zen rejects everything that has even the slightest to do with external teaching – it fosters absolute trust in a person's inner being. All truth in Zen comes from within.

Overlaying

Everything is the One Mind. There is nothing that could not be the One Mind. Solely in the way you face things and situations in the form of acceptance and rejection as habitual patterns of behaviour do you overlay reality with the delusions of your projections.

It is just as if in the evening moonlight you would see a snake lying across your path. You jump back horrified and run away. The next morning you return and realise – it was only an old rope.

Liberation from Ego-Delusion

Nowadays, there is much talk that you must kill your ego, the "I". Yet this is a completely wrong way of thinking, based on a total lack of understanding.

The truth is that no ego can be killed at all since in reality, no objective, bound "I" exists. Your notion of a personal self is your only bond.

Thus liberation can only take place when you liberate yourself from the delusion of a self, existing of its own accord. Each effort on the part of a supposed ego to kill itself would certainly achieve nothing but the opposite. It would only lead to a stronger attachment and an increase in inner resistance.

The Finger is not the Moon

The masters' words are like fingers that point to the moon. The moon is reality, the finger is merely the signpost. Yet you study the finger and cling to it.

You cannot find your true self through books and erudition since it is beyond all words – beyond all thought. You study the various doctrines, philosophies and religions and take that to be the truth. But it is all just worthless plunder, intellectual junk – nothing! The moon is the truth and not the finger.

The moment you suddenly awaken to the radiating reality of the Mind, you will perceive that all this was nothing more than chaff, without any further value.

Hocus-Pocus

Good and bad, yes and no, right and wrong are all phenomena of discriminating, conceptual thought.

Through these, the entire dream of a multitudinous, opposing world of phenomena arises. And you yourself, as the dreamer, are caught in your own hocus-pocus of a circle of birth and death within the illusion of space and time.

Behind this whole hocus-pocus of a projecting consciousness there is your true self – the One Mind.

The One Mind is like a cinema screen on which all projections, all images, all forms and all movements take place. However, the Mind itself remains untouched, regardless of what happens. It has nothing whatsoever to do with any of this.

Mirage

The entire external world of phenomena has only a relative existence, like for example a mirage, which you cannot just say is not there and does not exist.

You can actually see the mirage, this wonderful oasis with its refreshing spring and delightful plants. You see it, yet it is no more than a phenomenon, and thus has only a relative reality. In the same way, the whole world has only relative reality. All objects and all phenomena are but illusion.

The Mind is the sole reality, and beyond the Mind there exists nothing at all.

Mental Crutches

All of you are walking on mental crutches. You prop yourselves up with all sorts of lunacy just because you are afraid of walking without help. But Zen calls out for you to throw away your crutches.

Zen takes the sword of "non-discriminating realisation" and with one fell swoop slices through the Gordian knot of your spiritual confusion. The entire delusionary structure falls to pieces and the endless expanse of the One Mind shines forth. Indeed, this is exactly what makes Zen different from all other religious systems and philosophical teachings.

True Life Through Zen

True life through Zen means to retain a state of mind free from attachments, everywhere and constantly, so that you learn to deal with things in a non-identifying free way.

It is about learning to possess things without them possessing you. It is about acting without ego-relatedness, so that you are inwardly free of your actions. This is true life, out of, through, and in Zen.

Potter

Your thinking creates the karmic formational forces and thus the mental formations which activate all impulses of feeling and consequently, all sorts of notions.

In your imagination you can fabricate everything. It is just like with a potter. The potter has his clay from which he forms all sorts of things. Looking at his display, you see many different-shaped vessels: pitchers, bowls, cups, and all sorts of things, a remarkable assortment of forms. Yet all these different things are nothing but clay, just the same old clay.

The samskaras, your karmic formational forces, form the objects, but the substance, the clay, is the One Mind, beside which nothing else exists.

Wake up

Everything you devise or philosophically acquire through rational analysis and conceptual, discriminating thought is mere speculation and has nothing to do with the issue at hand.

By this, you fall ever deeper into mental confusion and distance yourself ever further from the clear light of the Mind which shines behind all experience as the uninvolved observer. This reality, beyond all thinking, is your true being.

Wake up! Stop dreaming – and the original state of your true being will shine forth in the light of Enlightenment, a hundred thousand times brighter than the sun.

In this boundless light the One Mind reveals itself as the sole existing reality, beside which nothing else exists.

Here and Now

In today's esoteric funfair, the expression "here and now" has become a worn out catchphrase.

"Here and now" can be found in almost every book of the esoteric wave, be it in the writings of modern western success-gurus or in the books and workshops of psychologists and therapists. Everyone talks about "here and now".

But when you really understand what Zen is all about, you will recognise that this whole esoteric "here and now talk" is utter nonsense and has nothing to do with the "here and now" of Zen, nothing whatsoever.

Here is Now! And that is eternity. You are always in eternity, even if you are not aware of it. Your thoughts produce the notion of time passing by.

Yet pure consciousness, "now-here", is beyond all changing. In the absolute presence of Here and Now, the Eternal reveals itself.

Esotericism

The esoteric funfair offers many methods which promise the spiritual seeker wonderful visions, mystical ecstasy, and powers to perform miracles. Yet all this belongs to the world of dreams and hot air. They are worldly phenomena, they are signs and miracles which dazzle only the ignorant.

All these artificial methods and doctrines that are supposed to work against delusion amount to no more than hocus-pocus – puffs of air in empty space.

That is why I say again and again, "Esotericism is only for dimwits."

Spiritual Bonds

Challenge all religious and philosophical dogmas! They are nothing more than interpretations of the neurotic mind. You need not believe in any religious dogma, whatever it may be. All teachings are dangerous since they can become dogmas and enchain the mind. Furthermore, your preoccupation with all sorts of teachings and artificial methods only leads to you wasting your precious time and squandering your spiritual energy.

There is nothing to learn, there is nothing to gain. Whoever believes there is something to seek is like a blind man in a dark room searching for a black cat which does not exist.

Divine Light

In the mysterious darkness of the cave of the heart, the light that we all seek reveals itself to us. Impenetrable to the senses and the intellect, it is the radiating splendour of our true self.

This light, experienced by the great mystics of all times and zones, of which the Gospel of St. John also speaks, is not only a symbol for the Divine as most Christian theologians proclaim today, but rather the direct self-revelation of divine reality.

All who have awakened to the reality of being beyond space and time have experienced God as light. Wherever a person is prepared to abandon himself out of love of the Divine, in complete relinquishment of his self, he will be granted the ascent of the inner light.

Mystical Darkness

Dying into the dark abyss of the divine void is an awakening to the reality of our true being. The "I" dissipates into the "dark night of the senses and the mind" and the true self experiences its resurrection in the eternal resplendence of its original being. Yet only when it has completely turned night in us will the inner sun arise. The greater the darkness, the brighter is the light that shines in us.

Cutting the Roots

To remove a tree, Zen does not start by clipping the smallest of the leaves. One little leaf and then another. And then there is another and yet another, and then the little twigs and so on, until reaching the bottom. Even before arriving at the bottom, everything has already grown back again at the top and you start all over again. This is not the way of Zen.

With the sword of non-discriminating realisation Zen fells the whole tree in a single stroke. Whack!

Be Here Now

What is it you want to achieve? There are no new possessions to acquire. Everything is present, here and now! In this instant, right here, the reality you seek reveals itself. It is neither in the past nor in the future.

Here and Now is eternity itself, and space and time are no more than a result of thinking, and thus illusion.

"Now", in this instant, be truly "here", without thoughts, without concepts and without ideas! Open yourself completely to this moment! This is the way of direct, instantaneous perception of reality, just as it is.

Intellect

You are so identified with your intellect that you do not even realise that it has made you its slave. Your identification with your intellect causes you to derive your self-esteem from it, and thus you fear that you will cease to exist if you stop thinking. The intellect always tries to attach and set limits because it can keep control of what is limited, and thus it can avoid opening itself and letting go.

But as long as you cling to your conditionings and the interwoven memories of your dead past and do not open yourself, you will never experience true joy. On the contrary: when divine joy catches sight of you it will hastily take flight.

Tail Stump

As long as you still try to free yourself of things, you will only go round in circles like a dog with a stumped tail trying to bite its stump. Round and round the dog goes, without success. However much you try in life to free yourself from the myriad things in this way, you will not be able to transcend birth and death.

Harmonic Unison

You live in unison with the world when you let everything take its natural course. Do not project your moral attitudes, conceptual fixations, behavioural patterns, all these conditionings onto everything you see, but instead let everything flow of its own accord.

Simply flow along with it! You walk through town and a pretty woman walks past who smiles at you, or you come across a teetering drunk who gabbles and swears at you.

Everything is good just as it is, for all is the one ocean of being. One wave is somewhat rounder, the other a little more pointed, another has a greater foam crest, and another has perhaps more bubbles. Yet everything is the one ocean. Everything is perfect.

Reflection

Just as a mirror only ever reflects the face that looks into it, so does the world you perceive only ever reflect your current state of consciousness. The world is just a reflection of your self and there is no point in blaming the reflection.

You cannot change the image of the world. You must begin with yourself if you wish to experience a joyful and peaceful world. This is an irrefutable spiritual law.

Letting Go

Only when you have freed yourself of all notions and thoughts of letting go can you awaken to the reality of the One Mind. Your letting go must become a forgetting of yourself and all things. You must forget everything: Buddha, Enlightenment, Dharma, Zen and whatever else it may be.

All these concepts are nothing other than empty words devoid of value. As long as you still cling to words, you can never reach a direct experience of your true being.

The Fullness of Being

As long as you do not truly live and truly breathe the joy of being, totally experiencing and feeling it in every pore of your body, you still remain caught in illusion.

And by joy, I am not talking about that external joy you only feel when things are going your way, when, for example, you are lying in bed with a beautiful woman or you are surrounded by a wonderful landscape, or a delightful meal is before you and you say: "Oh, how marvellous. What a wonderful world it is." – No!

"Every day is a good day," says Zen. Regardless of where you are, wherever it may be. Everywhere and constantly, the fullness of divine being reveals itself to you.

The Great Zen Way

The great Zen way is nothing for the small-minded. So why wait? Why say: "The Master gave another wonderful talk today and I'm getting closer still to what it's all about. Some things seem a little clearer, and someday ..."

Forget someday! There is no someday. Past and future are no more than thoughts that appear in the mind in the present moment.

The experience of time is thus nothing else than thinking, and all thinking is an erroneous belief and time is therefore nonexistent.

Imperishability

We are aware of the fact that our body has a beginning and is thus predestined to one day dissolve. Yet this does not pertain to our true self.

Our true self is unattached and unlimited and thus not touched by the changes of the world of phenomena to which this body with all its psychological aspects belongs.

Once we have recognised that the elements of existence which make up the delusion of a personality – corporeality, sensations, perceptions, mental formations, and consciousness – are not our true self, we no longer need fear their death – quite the contrary! The demise of the elements of existence would indeed mean the ascent of the inner light of the one who is free of all identifications.

Immerse Yourself

Personal experience is everything in Zen. There is no other way than to awaken to your true being. Wake up!

Stop dreaming and playing around in the sandbox of your conditionings! Stop viewing things solely through the template of your conceptual fixations, your social and moral attitudes, and saying: this is good and that is not good, this is right and that is wrong! There will be no end to it if you continue this way.

Right now in this instant, your original face reveals itself – nothing could be closer. Immerse yourself in it "now"! There is no other way.

Shatter Everything

Take the sword of non-discriminating wisdom and shatter everything, whatever it may be! Free yourself of all your tender notions! Be it Christianity, Hinduism, Buddhism, or whatever. Liberate yourself from all grafted-on ideals and free yourself from the burden of bygone illusions! Whether it be your notions of nirvana, of Enlightenment, or be it the entire world, no matter.

Zen is completely free and does not tolerate reliance on anything – not even on Buddha.

No Thinker

A thinker as subject does not exist. The thinker is nothing more than an accumulation of impressions, stored up since birth. Everything is merely occurrence! It is all just a psychic process! All that exists is a sequence of thoughts, based on pre-existing concepts.

When I say there is no thinker as subject, many people become afraid. Yet such fears are totally ungrounded, they merely betray attachment to something that does not exist.

Ego-Delusion

The thinker is no more than the sum of the thoughts. In other words, he is the thinking itself. There is no thinker separate from the thinking, however much you may still believe you are a static, continuous entity.

Essentially, there is nothing more than a rapid, complex succession of thoughts. This sum of rapid, sequential thoughts arouses in you the deceptive impression of an individual consciousness which acts within the illusion of space and time. Since this space-time limited consciousness erroneously believes it is something that lies beyond the thoughts, beyond the perceptions, it regards itself as being the centre of this whole business. And exactly that is the constant process of formation and perpetuation of the ego-delusion.

Only-Mind

Mind is not the opposite of matter as many believe, but rather it forms matter. It is its substance and thus the sole foundation of all that is material, that is, of all that is form.

All multiplicity is illusion! There is nought but a single being, the One Mind, beside which nothing else exists. It is the sole reality at the deepest ground of all living beings and of all things.

In truth, neither living beings nor objects exist separate from one another. Accordingly, material existence – the entire external world of phenomena, is just an illusion and a consequence of the perceiving consciousness.

Mind of Enlightenment

One of the central thoughts of Mahayana Buddhism is bodhichitta, "the Mind of Enlightenment". Bodhichitta means to strive for Enlightenment for the sake of the welfare of all living beings.

As long as a person strives for Enlightenment just for himself he will never attain Enlightenment. He can strive earnestly for countless incarnations but still he will not experience Enlightenment.

Breaking through to this liberating awakening precludes the profound awareness of the non-separateness of all beings. This requires the spiritual seeker to adopt a fundamental spiritual attitude which opens itself without limitations to life in its universality.

Such holistic openness embodies inner compassion for the pain and torment of all suffering beings.

Great Trust

All those who make serious efforts on the spiritual path also know the periods of disappointment, darkness, and unbelief, which vary in length.

Yet at the same time there is something that is there for us and remains, despite all doubt. It is that something that lets us know in our innermost self that that to which we have turned is nonetheless true. However, this trust is not the wavering trust of the beginner on the spiritual path but rather that great trust which has first to develop.

This unswerving trust is the faith which has opened itself in the innermost of the heart to the divine being and can never be lost. This faith stands solid on a rock.

Incertitude of the Hour of Death

The fact that one day we shall die is the highest certainty, and the highest uncertainty is the hour of death.

Death can suddenly take us by surprise, whether we are prepared for it or not. In that decisive moment, we will be forced to realise that all intellectual development, all power and all riches, everything we were devoted to in this life, can no longer give us the slightest aid or assurance.

When death touches us, there is nothing more that we can do. It tears everything from our hands. It destroys all possibilities we have for acting and planning, and it does it so fully and radically that everything that has gone before becomes nothing, as though it had never existed.

For the spiritual seeker it is therefore of the essence to practise the development of an attentiveness which constantly and in all of life's situations is aware of the incertitude of the hour of death.

Becoming Transparent

The more a person is prepared to surrender himself to the Absolute, the more he will be granted grace as the action of divine Essence. And the more it acts in him, the more he is capable of ever greater and steadfast self-surrender. Surrendering oneself to the Eternal means opening oneself and becoming transparent to the transcendental. It means letting go and becoming empty in the form of opening up to and thus becoming filled by the all-embracing wholeness of divine being.

The Pitfall of the Dead Void

Many people who practice meditation, especially Zen meditation, lead themselves to believe that true practice consists of stopping thoughts and suppressing the mind.

They allow themselves to be deceived and take this "pitfall of the dead void" to be the achievement of a higher state of immersion.

The result of this is that they often remain for long periods in this state, without realising how they have been lulled by the charms of the stillness of mind. Through this, their spiritual awareness becomes ever more dull and sluggish, instead of gaining in clarity.

True Zen-Meditation

The aim of true meditation is never to achieve a state of complete silence and relaxation with an utterly empty mind. Neither does it mean forcefully stopping and suppressing the mind.

True meditation means "becoming transparent to transcendence". It is the process of maturing towards a state of mind of being constantly aware of the presence of the totality of divine reality, which encompasses and fulfils us.

Grace

The inner encounter with the Divine is always a godsend and takes place solely through grace. All holy scriptures contain the term for grace and proclaim that Enlightenment and deliverance is only achievable through grace.

However, this action of divine grace cannot be forced by any meditation technique. The mystical experience of being touched and fulfilled by the Divine is always beyond a person's realm of control and cannot be brought about at a wish.

Whoever believes he need only apply certain meditation methods and will thus automatically achieve the goal of his spiritual striving is greatly deceived.

The great mystics, as authorities on the spiritual path, have constantly pointed out this error of spiritual materialism.

The Action of Divine Grace

We must not succumb to the aspiration that divine grace will lay touch on us through some blind fancy. We should not expect that we need only ask for grace or even that we can force it with some "New Age technique" of positive thinking.

If we wish to be blessed with grace as the working of divine love, there is no other way than for us to withdraw ourselves in our actions and our wanting, so that divine love can act in us.

Active Meditation

The practice of Zen meditation does not only involve sitting in silence on the meditation cushion but moreover in the way you fulfil everything in a state of awareness and are completely present in all things. Therefore, we can say that Zen meditation reveals itself in everything: sitting, walking, standing and lying down – in all that you do.

The fruits of Zen can only be reached when, by forgetting ourselves and all things, we step out of the realm of practice and single-minded wanting into the realm where we leave all practice far behind us.

Inner Demons

Your discriminating, conceptual thinking causes your self-made demons to appear, along with the whole satanic realm of greed, hatred and blindness.

However, these demons are not real, substantial beings. Rather, they are conditioned, and thus negative thought-associations which have become autonomous. They are brought forth by the ego-delusion and do not have an existence of their own, independent of the mind.

Whoever can truly recognise this, can transform his inner demons into the pure, crystal-clear awareness of the Mind.

Clinging On

As long as you still so cling to life that you think, "I want to die into the divine abyss but I hope I'll return to life", you are not yet mature enough for mystical death – for Enlightenment. You just go round and round in circles and lose yourself in the entanglement of your spiritual confusion.

You can only experience the reality of divine being when you completely die into it, radically, without remainder. And that means that you must let go so entirely that indeed, you completely forget yourself and all things.

Challenge

Each moment we live is a divine gift and a unique opportunity for realisation, for no one knows whether he will still be able to draw his next breath.

Fully aware of this fact, no true master will waste his time with polite chit-chat, aimed at uplifting the student. Instead, he will be a constant challenge for the student, who, as long as he is yet to penetrate the hidden tricks of his ego, will feel extremely misunderstood and hurt.

Purification

A master will constantly aim to push the student to the limit of his possibilities.

Again and again he will prompt his student to rid himself of all clouds of unknowing, attachment and illusion. He will snatch away all props from him so that he awakens to his true self, divested of all things. He will edge him onwards by all available means right up to the abyss of hopelessness, so that the student has no other option than to "let go" or cling tightly with all his might to his dreamworld.

But no matter how the master treats his student, it is all for the sake of fostering the process of spiritual maturing. Behind all apparent rigour there lies the master's great love of his student, with whom he completely empathises.

And yet, in the long run, this arduous purification process is only for those who are really serious about it and are ready to put everything at stake for the truth – even if it is their own life.

Love of the Eternal

Whoever, out of love of the Eternal, lets go of the small temporal life, likewise thus opens himself to the great life beyond space and time which is waiting for him.

The presence of that which exists concealed within us in our innermost self then becomes a vivacious, inner experience. However, we can only experience this to the extent that we are receptive to it and prepared to let go of our self and all things. By casting off yourself and all things, you free yourself from that deadly self-confidence which is the sign of the earth-bound worldly person who, lacking in faith, is more likely to place his trust in himself than in God.

Fear of Death

A person's greatest fear of death is the fear of ceasing to exist. He fears that at the moment of death he will become nothing. Most people believe that their entire existence comprises a single lifespan, which begins at the moment of birth and ends at the time of death.

The fear of ceasing to exist is based solely on the misconception that you are born from nothing and in dying, you return to nothing. In his fear of his unavoidable eradication, a person avoids everything that could remind him of death.

Yet whoever excessively clings to his mundane life is only showing that he is still dominated by his small "I". Since a life within the bounds of space and time constitutes the only tangible reality of being for him, he clings tightly to the "I", which at this level, he continues to equate with his own life. This clasping is the real cause of his fear of death.

Pure Love

Pure love is love in the form of all-embracing wholeness. It constantly seeks to remove all opposites, for it constantly strives towards consummate oneness.

Pure love does not remain attached to the conditioned sentimental impulse of dualistic discrimination. It is not pseudo-love, which wishes to grasp and possess, but quite the opposite. It is true love which gives of itself and surrenders itself. Just like the moth that, on seeing the open fire, forgetting itself, flies into the fire and becomes transformed in it.

Spiritual Blindness

The ego has no existence of its own, rather it is merely a process. It is a process in the form of identification with the memories of a dead past, with old patterns of behaviour and with countless notions and concepts.

But that is not what you are. That has not the slightest to do with what you really are at the ground of your being.

Yet in your spiritual blindness you nonetheless believe this to be you, and are convinced that all others are this way too. What is more, you believe the external world to be what your senses perceive.

In truth, you only appear to perceive external things through your sense organs, for space is no more than a projection of consciousness.

You may believe you are moving in a three-dimensional world of space and time, but in fact it is only the mind that moves. The mind is the fundament of everything, and everything takes place only in the mind.

The Sword of Awareness

Look directly at your desire to think in terms of concepts, and your autonomous thinking will dissolve of its own accord. With all thoughts that arise, it is important that you directly examine your desire to think. Without relating to it, just look at everything which takes place in the mind.

In this way you will be able to instantly cut through each current of thought with the sword of complete awareness of mind.

The moment the thoughts no longer receive any sustenance, that is, when they are no longer taken heed of, they dissolve like snowflakes in warm water.

Rooted in Tao

When one has returned to his true, original nature, his whole being resides in harmonious unison with the all-embracing wholeness of existence. It reveals itself in the nature of a bird; it sings out of inner freedom and lives in coessential harmony with heaven.

He who is rooted in Tao and lives this way, in unison with the harmonious movement of heaven, thus becomes a revelation of Tao in the midst of the world and gains immortality beyond death.

Wu-Wei

Wu-wei, non-action, transcends both extremes: restless activity and absolute inactivity. It is a non-abiding in the voidness, which at the same time allows the essential to take effect.

This means that in each situation where action is necessary we withdraw ourselves such that the universal effect of the Tao acts through us, so that our whole activity becomes an "acting without action".

Genderless Ascetic

A person who has achieved spiritual realisation is no solemn, genderless ascetic, as proponents of dualistic belief preach. Indeed, those who reject and suppress sexual energy turn their backs on life itself and, according to tantric truth, will never be capable of attaining a higher, all-embracing spiritual realisation. Those who suppress their sexuality rather than transform it, only end up causing it to circle within them, finding no outlet and finally manifesting itself in some abnormal way.

The Wave is the Ocean

There is only one single problem, and that is you yourself. You are the problem for the simple reason that this individual which you believe yourself to be does not exist at all. For in reality, the "I", the ego, is nothing more than an object in the judgement of discriminating thinking.

There is no individual personality, distinguishing itself from other individual personalities, just as there is no wave which distinguishes itself from all other waves on the surface of the ocean.

Everything is the one ocean, just as everything is the One Mind, beside which nothing else exists, in its all-encompassing wholeness.

Important Incarnations

In Zen it is necessary that you cast off false understanding and wrong perception, so that you see through the deceptive nature of all phenomena.

But by not perceiving the voidness of all phenomena you identify yourself with your old thought patterns and then believe: this is the world and this is my personality.

For that reason, all of you who come here to me are very considerable personalities – important incarnations. Each of you is something very special.

Multidimensional Perspective

I am I and you are you. This is the discriminating, dualistic way of looking at things of an average worldly-bound person. "I am you and you are me, whoever sees me sees us, in our self we enfold the universe." This is the multidimensional perspective of an enlightened being.

This is the cosmic dimension of the all-embracing whole, for all apparent multiplicity is an organic all-embracing whole, complete in itself, which contains everything within it.

God is Love

Reality beyond being is the all-embracing wholeness of being. It is the entirety which contains everything within itself. It is the one inseparable whole, which recognises and loves itself in all apparent multiplicity.

God, or in the language of Zen: the One Mind, is love. And whoever abides in this love – in this whole, in this non-duality, in this non-separateness – abides in the reality of the One Mind, and the reality of the One Mind in him.

But the moment you take anything away, believing it does not belong to the total harmony of being, you also step out of love. You lose love and thus God.

Yet whoever abides in love, abides in God and God in him.

Love is Stronger than Death

Just as death tears you away from everything and annihilates everything, so too does love. Whoever abides in all-embracing love experiences everything as this pure love.

He now sees nothing but the Divine, he sees nothing but pure reality wherever he goes, wherever he stands, everywhere. When you abide in this love, you are beyond life and death, for everything is then One.

The whole universe, coming and going, life and death – everything, whatever it may be, is the fullness of pure being. And if you live in and from this fullness of eternal being, you are free of all anxiety and fear.

Then death is not the final word. It is no longer this dark menace which will tear you away from your life for you to fall into a dark empty nothingness.

As the hand of divine love, it raises you up into the blazing light of the Mind, into the reality of your birthless and deathless Self-Nature.

Glowing Fairy-tale Flowers

You need not go anywhere to find the highest truth. Tao lies beneath the soles of your feet.

Stop projecting and entangling yourself in the creeping snarl of your discriminating, conceptual thinking! Open your eyes and be present! Be aware in everything that you do! If you are truly aware in everything that you do, the reality of your true being reveals itself to you – just as it is.

Then, the whole world transforms for you into a radiant paradise with a wonderful array of magnificently glowing fairy-tale flowers.

The True Way

The true way of Zen has nothing to do with knowledge, nor has it anything to do with ignorance. However, this does not mean that it is just fine for you not to understand the way.

If you take your ignorance for granted, you continue to live the mentally deranged life of an average worldly-bound person. Like the majority of people, you eke out your miserable existence in indifferent non-consciousness.

If, on the other hand, you are convinced in all seriousness that you are capable of understanding Tao, the true way, then you are truly in a lamentable state of hopeless confusion.

The true way is beyond knowledge and ignorance, it is the everyday mind, completely free of all acceptance and rejection.

The Heart of the Selfhood

The question of Self and Being is ultimately a question of our "Self-Being". However, this question can only be answered when we transcend the realm of separation and perceive our true self as the mutual self of all beings. For since the same Being is the heart of the selfhood of every individual, there can be no delimited individuality, existing of its own.

When a person turns inwards and therein lets go of his self and all things, himself now having become that which he was seeking, he will perceive nothing other than that which "is" – the Self-Being, existing of and out of its self.

No Thoughts – No Problems

When thoughts arise and turn autonomous then all notions and feelings arise too. All concepts arise, together with their resulting patterns of behaviour, and therefore all problems. And when thoughts cease, all self-induced problems cease too. Then, the reality of the radiating One Mind, which has constantly been present behind this entanglement as your true being, reveals itself to you in its entire splendour.

Fear of the Void

The fear of emptying the mind and falling into the void is what results when you cannot see through the deceptive nature of all phenomena and the attachment it leads to.

However, when you suddenly realise that all phenomena, the entire universe, everything, whatever it may be, is the indivisible One Mind in the form in which it appears to you – what is left for you to fear?

This One Mind is the source of all life. It is the life which gives life to all life and therefore is life itself. What does the water drop have left to fear when it falls into the great ocean and dissolves into it, thus experiencing itself as the endless ocean? Your fear of the void originates solely from the fact that you do not know that your own mind is the One Mind, and thus the void.

A Life Without Chains

Let nothing, whether it be so holy and full of philosophical wisdom, come between you and the direct, immediate experience of your true being!

Zen is the most free and most direct teaching, in which there is nothing to do and nothing to learn. Zen is a life without bonds, a life in freedom, and is freedom itself. Therefore, shatter the self-made chains of your grasping, inconsequential "I" – and your true self will shine resplendent in its entire grandeur, all-embracing and all-pervading!

A Muzzlefull of Old Rubbish

All thought is an erroneous belief, says Zen. So why stuff your brain with all sorts of intellectual rubbish? What is the point of rooting around in every corner like a dog which scrapes up all kinds of old rubbish in its muzzle? Dig into your own treasure, for the truth you are seeking is closer to you than you are to yourself.

There is nothing to seek, there is nothing to gain! There is no space in which things could be separate from one another, and there is no time in which anything is yet to happen or has already taken place. For everything is a simultaneity, revealing itself in this instance "now-here".

Divine Self

The eternally radiating light of the One Mind is our original true being. It is our intrinsic, immortal self. It is completely detached from the various forms in which beings appear, bound in space and time, and their multitudinous forms of existence.

In contrast, the ignorant, vagrant ego is nothing more than a shadow which disappears at the moment of Enlightenment, when the splendour of the divine Self radiates forth.

Mystical Death

As paradox as it may seem, the death and demise of the clasping little "I" is the ascent of the true self. What we experience in the process of mystical death as dying, manifests itself as the transition from death to life. Mystical death reveals itself as the great resurrection.

The great death and the great life are one and the same. Totally letting go and dissolving into the fullness of divine being is "one" experience and takes place in the same instant. It is the great moment of awakening from the dream of an assumed world of multitude.

By breaking through to our true being, we are raised above all limitations of a worldly-bound human existence and we experience our ascent above the dark haze of phenomena into the clear light of reality.

The wall of death has been penetrated, "the curtain of the temple tears and reveals the Holy of Holies".

Don't Put Off

All of us know that someday we must die, but most of us have pushed far aside the notion of the possibility that death can come now, within the hour.

However, it is a fact that one's life force can vanish as fast as a dew drop falls from the tip of the blade of grass. A person's life is as easy to destroy as a soap bubble.

Therefore, it is a fatal error and gross stupidity to put off your practise on the spiritual path by arguing that you are currently much too busy, and by claiming that later you will begin with the spiritual path when you have more time.

Contact

ZEN-ZENTRUM
TAO 道 CHAN

Tao Chan Zentrum e.V.
Adelheidstr. 37
D-65185 Wiesbaden
Germany

The Tao Chan Zen Center is under the personal direction of Zen-Master Zensho W. Kopp.
During his many years as an active spiritual master, a large community of students has come together whom he regularly instructs.

Zen-Sesshin

Twice a month, Zen Master Zensho leads a Zen-day where guests may participate.

Information and registration

Tel. +49 (0)611 940 623 -1
www.tao-chan.org
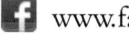 www.facebook.com/zencentertaochan

ZENSHO W. KOPP

The Freedom of Zen
The Zen book
that shatters all limits
and bounds

216 pages, 12,95 €
ISBN 978-3-83916-893-6
paperback
Print on Demand
Available at www.tao-chan.org

This inspiriting book is a total rebellion against the intellect. It smashes our well-worn views and all of our fond illusions. Zen Master Zensho shows how we can free ourselves of the slavery of autonomous compulsive thinking and how we can experience the enlightened state of pure consciousness.

Uncompromisingly, everything is swept away so we become able to reach that boundless freedom of the Mind which lies beyond everything that sense and reason can comprehend.

Zensho's humorous geniality and his free unconventional way of conveyance bestow a tremendous vitality on his talks. His clear words are a vivid and direct revelation of the great simplicity and freedom of Zen.

An exceptional book by an exceptional Zen Master.

ZENSHO W. KOPP

Lao-tse, Tao Te King
The holy book of Tao

Transcription
by Zensho W. Kopp

110 pages, 7,95 €
ISBN 978-3-8423-2861-7
paperback
Print on Demand
Available at www.tao-chan.org

The 2500 year old Tao Te King by the Chinese sage Lao-tse is a jewel of Eastern wisdom. It counts as one of the most profound and most translated books of world literature.

In a language of incomparable imagery the Tao Te King speaks of the Tao, the divine origin of all existence, and its effect in man as true virtue. Its goal is to lead him back to the original oneness with the Tao, and so into harmony with the all-embracing wholeness of existence.

In this outstanding new transcription, Zensho has succeeded in masterly conveying the whole mystical expressiveness of the work whilst strictly adhering to the original sense, and thus providing a completely new and deeper insight.

A timeless book of wisdom, unique mysteriousness, and linguistic beauty.